A Commoner's View: The Application of Operational Art in Counterinsurgency Operations

A Monograph
by
MAJ Drew R. Conover
United States Army

MENS EST CLAVIS VICTORIAE

School of Advanced Military Studies
United States Army Command and General Staff College
Fort Leavenworth, Kansas

AY 2010-11

Abstract

A COMMONER'S VIEW: THE APPLICATION OF OPERATIONAL ART IN COUNTERINSURGENCY OPERATIONS by MAJ Drew R. Conover, United States Army, 51 pages.

The marked changed in the types of wars fought over the last ten years in Afghanistan and Iraq have demonstrated the need for commanders at echelons below the campaign level to develop and continuously refine operational approaches to guide their decisions and tactical actions within an assigned area of operation. Modern doctrine and most military literature regarding these wars have been deficient in fully explaining the significance of this new requirement and fail to recognize this as the application of operational art. The monograph explores this issue by investigating the concept of operational art and its application in modern counterinsurgency operations.

The monograph demonstrates that U.S. counterinsurgency operations aim to achieve stability within an extremely complex environment. Because of this complexity, units must develop unique approaches and tailor solutions to the many different local areas. As such, subordinate commands employ operational art to achieve local stability by developing and refining long term plans that drive the development and execution of tactical action.

Modern Army doctrine should refine its definition of operational art to reflect the essence of this concept. The findings also highlight the need for further research on synchronizing the application of operational art across multiple levels of command.

Table of Contents

Introduction

The introduction of operational art in U.S. Army doctrine in 1986 marked a profound shift in American military thought. This operational concept underlying AirLand battle served as a guide to fighting the Soviet Union and clearly reflected the accepted concepts and the context of the environment in which it was created. Tactically, it addressed the challenges of projecting forces to another continent while simultaneously fighting an opponent with significant advantages in manpower and resources. Strategically, it served to remedy the failure in Vietnam by properly aligning policy, strategy, and the military campaign to achieve national success.[1]

The last ten years, however, have demonstrated a marked shift in the character of war from major combat operations to counterinsurgency operations. Conducting campaigns and operations in the counterinsurgency environment is qualitatively different in many respects. In response, U.S. Army doctrine has changed significantly to ensure that it is useful in guiding actions in the modern environment. Where doctrine has not changed is in its descriptions of operational art and the operational level of war, which still remain heavily influenced by concepts associated with major combat operations. The monograph seeks to address the absence of change by asking the question, does operational art apply to counterinsurgency operations and if so, who should be doing it? The monograph argues that operational art is not only applicable to counterinsurgency operations, but that it can be employed by lower echeloned commands assigned permanent areas of operations.

The Operational Level of War Defined

A working definition of operational art and the operational level of war must first be addressed to lay the foundation for investigating this hypothesis. Underlying these definitions is

---

[1] John S. Brown, "The Maturation of Operational Art: Operations Desert Shield and Desert Storm" in *Historical Perspectives of the Operational Art* (Washington, D.C: U.S. Army Center for Military History, 2007), 439-440.

1

the nature of policy and its interdependency with war. Military theorist Carl von Clausewitz famously describes war as an extension of politics by other means.[2] This statement is significant because it bounds military action to policy, thereby providing the context within which war is waged. The aims of policy are always to seek advantageous positions, as opposed to victory, because interaction will always occur between the opposing nations in some form.[3] This suggests that the way in which the military accomplishes its objectives is important to ensure that military actions do not hinder or limit the nation's ability to effectively interact with the opposing nation in the future. Thus, the political authorities define the type of war the military will fight and impose restrictions to prevent military action from producing harmful political effects.[4] Additionally, military action will inherently create unforeseen strategic challenges and reveal new information which may lead to the refinement of strategy and policy. Therefore, political authorities must be closely integrated with military planners to ensure military action both supports and informs policy.

Larger and more intense wars in the 19th and 20th centuries prevented political authorities from focusing solely on the conduct of military operations due to the critical importance of the evolving homeland functions required to sustain and prosecute wars. The role of the campaign commander gradually evolved to include both political and strategic discourse to enable a common understanding, and possibly refinement, of what is to be achieved politically and what can be achieved tactically. The campaign command thus came to serve three primary functions. First, it provides the tactical perspective to the development of strategy and policy. Second, it unifies a wide range of capabilities under one common purpose to ensure that tactical actions are

---

[2] Carl von Clausewitz, *On War*, 1st Edition ed. (Princeton, N.J.: Princeton University Press, 1989), 87.

[3] Everett Dolman, *Pure Strategy: Power and Policy in the Space and Information Age*, (New York: Routledge, 2005), 14-15.

[4] Colin S. Gray, *War, Peace and International Relations: An Introduction to Strategic History* (New York: Routledge, 2008), 10-11.

purposeful in achieving the ends of policy and strategy.[5] Finally, it integrates and assists in the sustainment of the wide array of forces participating in the campaign. This unique function came to be known in the United States military as the operational level of war.

Operational Art Defined

The purpose of the campaign is to achieve the strategic aim. Because of the complexities and uncertainties that exist in any long term human endeavor, a strategic aim must be general and conceptually based because what is possible to achieve is heavily influenced by the second and third order effects of the actions taken along the way. The effects of these actions simply cannot be predicted with any precision at the beginning of the conflict because of the unlimited interdependent variables in the environment.[6] Therefore, the campaign commander generates a broad, long range plan, or operational approach, to guide decision making and selection of short term objectives to progress towards the strategic aim.[7]

These short term objectives are the intermediate, or operational, objectives. Strategic thought is used to determine, with the information currently available, which intermediate objectives best contribute to the achievement of the strategic aim. Further, an analysis of the various methods to achieve these intermediate objectives must also be considered. This is significant because the methods, or tactical actions selected to accomplish objectives, will have second and third order effects which will impact the strategic context in various ways. Thus, operational art requires strategic thought to develop the operational approach, select intermediate objectives, and select methods for achieving those objectives.

---

[5] Ibid. 17-18

[6] Huba Wass de Czege, "Thinking and Acting Like an Explorer: Operational Art Is Not a Level of War," *Small Wars Journal* (14 March 2011): 3, http://smallwarsjournal.com (accessed March 21, 2011).

[7] Smith, 17.

Operational art also requires tactical thought and short term planning to determine how best to achieve these intermediate objectives in an effective and efficient manner given the strategic constraints.[8] The goal of the tactician is to overwhelmingly defeat the opponent while simultaneously preventing him from doing the same. Military action involves killing and thus the tactician is intimately concerned with effective and efficient application of force to bring the engagement to a rapid conclusion to preserve both the moral and combat power of the force.[9]

In addition to aligning short term, intermediate objectives with the strategic aim, the inherent difficulty for the operational artist is also accomplishing intermediate objectives in a highly efficient manner while ensuring that the effects of these actions contribute positively to the higher strategic aim. This is the cognitive tension inherent in the practice of operational art. Adhering to what is best to achieve the strategic aim can prevent the tactician from accomplishing the assigned mission in the most efficient or effective manner possible. In extreme cases, these restrictions can potentially render tactical victory unattainable. This cognitive tension is a defining feature of operational art and must be continually negotiated as intermediate objectives are attained and new ones developed.

As the intermediate objectives are attained, additional information becomes available which may cause a change in planned future objectives, the refinement of the operational approach, or potentially the strategic aim. Thus, analysis must be conducted to reassess the military, political, and social variables between opponents prior to executing the next step. Therefore, operational art is an iterative process of taking small steps, refining the approach given the new information, then taking another step. Thus, operational art, in its most basic form, is the cognitive, cyclical process, using both strategic and tactical thought, to develop and refine an

---

[8] Wass de Czege, 2-4.

[9] Rupert Smith, *The Utility of Force: The Art of War in the Modern World (Vintage)* (New York: Vintage, 2008), 16 and Everett Dolman, *Pure Strategy: Power and Policy in the Space and Information Age (Strategy and History)*, New ed. (New York: Routledge, 2005), 9.

operational approach to guide the selection of appropriate tactical actions aimed at the simultaneous achievement of intermediate objectives and strategic aims.

Methodology

The monograph explores three keys areas. It first identifies the critical elements and defining features of operational art which make it unique from other forms of planning. It then investigates the nature of counterinsurgency operations to determine if, and to whom, this process is applicable in this type of war. Finally, the monograph explains how the findings impact the United States' preparation for, and execution of, counterinsurgency operations.

Chapters One and Two examine the essence of operational art within the context of maneuver warfare. These chapters demonstrate how, in this type of warfare, operational art is applied almost exclusively by the campaign, or operational level of war. This is critical because traditional literature has studied the concept of operational art primarily within maneuver warfare. This in turn continues to inhibit the military's ability to apply this concept in other types of war as operational art and maneuver warfare have almost become synonymous terms. Chapter Two concludes by determining that the concept of operational art, translating strategic aims into tactical action, is applicable in any type of war and therefore, does apply to counterinsurgency operations.

Given that operational art applies to counterinsurgency operations, the purpose of chapter two is to determine who should be using the operational art process in this type of war. It first establishes the context of counterinsurgency operations to demonstrate the complexity within the environment and the challenges confronting the many commands operating in a decentralized manner. Given the context of the environment, the central focus of the chapter is on the nature of the strategic aim and the objectives assigned to subordinate commanders. This analysis reveals whether campaign objectives are met in a linear fashion, as in major combat operations, or if the strategic aim is achieved in a fundamentally different manner. Further, it details what subordinate commands are being asked to do in such an environment and whether these tasks are distinctly different than those assigned in major combat operations. The chapter concludes by determining that operational art should be applied by lower echeloned commands assigned permanent areas of operations.

Chapter three addresses the significance of the monograph's findings. It first analyzes doctrine to determine its usefulness in explaining the application of the operational concepts to counterinsurgency operations. It then addresses the education and training system changes necessary within the Army to prepare the officer corps to employ operational art at lower levels. The chapter concludes by addressing the implications of these findings with respect to the actual conduct of operations in counterinsurgency.

Chapter 1: 19th Century Warfare and Operational Art

The purpose of this chapter is to provide the foundation for analyzing the essence of the operational concepts in the context of maneuver warfare. Maneuver warfare is significant because it has historically been the focus area for the study of the operational concepts in military history and heavily influenced the development and current description of the operational concepts in modern doctrine. The chapter analyzes two 19th century campaigns, Napoleon at Jena and the American Civil War in 1864, to demonstrate the first signs of a new, emerging type of warfare that came to dominate military operations in the 20th century. However, the chapter refrains from the detailed discussions of the precise characteristics of each of the dominant forms of maneuver in an effort to focus on the essence of operational art. Additionally, the chapter focuses on the various levels of command which employed operational art throughout the 19th century to highlight how these periods shaped the warfare in the 20th century and the United States Army's modern understanding of the terms.

Napoleonic Warfare

The Napoleonic era of the early 19th century marked the final period of warfare prior to the onset of the industrial revolution and the rise of most national armies. Communications and logistics during this period played a significant part in the both the political-military dynamic and the conduct of war. The communications networks consisted mostly of horse courier or word of mouth. Horses generally traveled at a rate of 5-10 mph while word of mouth could travel up to 250 miles in one day. However, word of mouth communication was often unreliable at best as the information was passed verbally through many different people over great distances.[10] Therefore, if rulers or political leaders did not accompany their men to the field of battle, they relinquished nearly all strategic and political control to the operational commander because continuous dialogue could not be maintained to stay abreast with the changing strategic situation resulting from tactical action.[11]

Equally as important were logistical operations. Supplies during this time period consisted mostly of food and fodder which could be collected nearly anywhere the army moved. Additionally, cash was collected from the occupied territory to both pay the soldiers and buy additionally supplies. Therefore, a military force could generally sustain itself for a significant period of time and was not forced to rely upon domestic lines of communication in large measure.

These two characteristics of the period meant that if the political objective of war was important, the king or political leader was generally free to leave the home front and accompany the army onto the field of battle.[12] The campaigns of Napoleon in the early 19th century highlight this important point as he simultaneously served as the emperor of France, the military strategist, and the campaign commander. Therefore, he was present on the field of battle to make key

---

[10] Martin Van Creveld, *Command in War* (Cambridge: Harvard University Press, 1985), 12, 87.

[11] Ibid., 20.

[12] Ibid., 59.

political and strategic decisions and guide the conduct of the campaign as tactical engagements changed the strategic situation. Therefore, the operational level of war did not exist in the Napoleonic system.

Although there was not an operational level of war during this time period, the application of operational art is clearly evident and took the form of "classical warfare". In short, "classical warfare", most notably demonstrated by the Napoleonic campaigns in the 1800s, was identified with the maneuvering of large, condensed corps to place forces in a position of advantage prior to a single, decisive battle.[13] Rather than maneuver the army along one avenue of approach, Napoleon marched his corps along multiple axes, each within one day's travel of each other. This form of maneuver provided flexibility at the campaign level to permit relatively rapid responses to the uncertain location of enemy formations and to converge on multiple positions to set conditions for the final battle. Simultaneously, it increased the pace at which the campaign advanced by avoiding unnecessary congestion along a single road.[14] The final battle was characterized by the concentration of force from multiple positions of advantage against the consolidated enemy formation to destroy his army or force his capitulation.

The Jena campaign is a prime example of the operational art process. Napoleon marched three corps along multiple axis of advance aimed at the destruction of the Prussian army. However, it was his constant refinement of the operational approach, as intermediate objectives were attained, that makes this process significant. Napoleon ultimately defeated the Prussian army at Jena and Austerlitz simultaneously through the conduct of two major operations.[15] This was not his original plan. Rather, it was the result of the gradual realization of a conceptual aim

---

[13] Dr. James J. Schneider, *Vulcan's Anvil: The American Civil War and the Foundation of Operational Art   Theoretical Paper No. Four* (Fort Leavenworth: United States Army Command and General Staff College, 10 May 2004), 30.

[14] David D. Chandler, "Napolean, Operational Art, and the Jena Campaign" in *Historical Perspectives of the Operational Art* (Washington, D.C: U.S. Army Center for Military History, 2007), 32-34.

[15] Van Creveld, p.78-95

8

over time by seizing opportunities revealed by tactical action at intermediate stages of the campaign. Each major action revealed new information which enabled a deeper understanding of the strategic context, and thus refinement of the operational approach.

Significant to this form of warfare was the corps system. The corps were the tools by which Napoleon executed his campaign. These corps were the forces that accomplished the near term tactical objectives within the operational approach outlined in the campaign plan. Thus, operational art was employed exclusively by Napoleon at the campaign level as the subordinate corps executed tactical planning against near term objectives with definitive ends. This form of operational art remained the dominant operational concept through much of the American Civil War fifty years later.

The American Civil War

Two significant events merged during the American Civil War to change the both the size and methods of maneuver warfare over the next century. The rise of mass armies, first seen in France under Napoleon, meant that there were significantly more troops, resources, and national will required to fight and win a war. The industrial revolution, which enabled the mass production of the steam engine, railroad, and telegraph, allowed for the employment of these massive forces over much greater distances with more flexibility.[16] As a consequence, the Napoleonic intent of forcing a decision in one major battle became obsolete and was unattainable during the American Civil War due to the size of armies and the dispersion of these forces across the theater.

Because armies were much larger, heavily reliant on technology, and forced to fight more than one large battle, full mobilization of the nation's resources was required to sustain the war.[17]

---

[16] William A. Murray, "The Industrialization of War 1815-71," in *The Cambridge Illustrated History of Warfare,* ed. Geoffrey Parker, (Cambridge: Cambridge University Press, 2008), 220.

[17] Dr. James J. Schneider, *Theoretical Paper No. Four: Vulcan's Anvil: The American Civil War and the Foundation of Operational Art,* 34.

This marks a key turning point in the evolution of the operational concept as political officials were now, more than ever, tied to the supporting rear due to the importance of managing the necessary homeland functions required to sustain and effectively prosecute the war. Additionally, the military strategist was positioned with the political authority to provide military advice and stay abreast with changes in policy. Therefore, a significant change in the structure of war planning occurred and a new level of responsibility emerged, the operational level of war.

At this level, the campaign commander became responsible for engaging in political and strategic discourse and providing a tactical perspective to the development of strategy and refinement of political ends. Additionally, the operational level provided the control mechanism for integrating, supporting, and employing the large number of forces now required to fight and win the war by way of the campaign plan. The campaign plan, in turn, unified all tactical action under one common purpose to achieve those strategic aims.[18] General Ulysses S. Grant performed this new function as the theater commander working between President Lincoln and General Halleck, the military strategist, while simultaneously controlling the armies subordinate to the campaign.[19] Additionally, U.S. Grant was instrumental in shifting the strategic aim from destroying the Confederate army to forcing its collapse, otherwise known as an indirect approach.

The new strategic aim highlights the application of operational art in the later part of the Civil War. Forcing the collapse of the Confederacy was an abstract and general concept. It required a broad approach and consistent refinement of intermediate objectives to ultimately achieve this aim. Specifically, Grant sought to isolate the southern armies from their resource base in Atlanta and Richmond.[20] Utilizing the full capacity of the telegraph and railroad, he

---

[18] Ibid., 14-15.

[19] Brooks D. Simpson, *Ulysses S. Grant: Triumph Over Adversity, 1822-1865* (Boston: Houghton Mifflin Harcourt, 2000), 272-274.

[20] Shimon Naveh, Jim Schneider, and Timothy Challans, *The Structure of Operational Revolution: A Prolegomena* (Leavenworth: Booz Allen Hamilton Inc., 2009), 44-46.

employed a number of major independent operations throughout the depth of the Confederate states to initially destroy critical infrastructure and their will to fight.[21] As the Union armies came within supporting distance of each other, Grant directed the simultaneously convergence of two armies on Atlanta and another two on Richmond, each with supporting tasks of isolating the city while the other army seized it.[22] The important distinction is the gradual steps taken by the campaign to bring about the collapse of the south. Not clearly evident at the start of the campaign, Grant refined the intermediate objectives and methods for achieving those objectives as tactical action changed the strategic situation. Thus, it was an iterative process which unified subordinate action under one purpose to simultaneously accomplish intermediate objectives and achieve the strategic aim.

The tools Grant used to execute his campaign plan were the field armies subordinate to the campaign.[23] However, these armies operated under different conditions than those experienced by the corps under Napoleon. They were separated by vast distances of hundreds of miles. Further, their initial guidance of destroying critical infrastructure was somewhat abstract as well. Because of this, these units likely employed long term planning that drove tactical decisions and selection of intermediate objectives during the initial phases of the campaign. Thus, operational art was employed by the subordinate armies as well. During the final phase of the campaign, the attacks on Richmond and Atlanta, these armies executed tactical tasks with definitive ends. Therefore, they employed a tactical planning model during this phase.

The Impacts of Early Maneuver Warfare on Operational Planning

Maneuver warfare and the operational concepts emerged from the dramatic social and technological innovations of the 19th century. The Napoleonic Wars served as one of the last

---

[21] Ibid., 44-46

[22] Ibid., 47-48.

[23] Dr. James J. Schneider, *Theoretical Paper Number 3: The Theory of Operational Art*, 15.

periods in warfare where a national ruler could also serve as the military strategist and campaign commander, thus the marking the absence of the operational level of war. Further, this period highlights the origins of operational art in maneuver warfare as strategic aims were now achieved through a series of sequential and simultaneous operations, as opposed to the traditional idea of fighting only one major battle.

The American Civil War highlights the origin of the operational level of war, as politicians and military strategists were occupied with homeland functions required to sustain and prosecute the war. Additionally, the application of operational art at the campaign level became more complex as the strategic aim changed and armies regenerated at a much quicker rate. No longer could an entire army be destroyed. Rather, the Union Army sought creative solutions to force the collapse of the Confederate Army by isolating their forces from their resource base. This became known as the indirect approach.

The form of operational art introduced in the American Civil War, outflanking the front lines and conducting major operations in the enemy rear, became the dominant mode of thought for many countries leading into World War I. Although this technique failed catastrophically in the coming war, it did highlight the important integration of technology and the idea of linking operations in depth from the supporting rear to the fighting front, a key concept in the Russian Deep Operations theory.

Chapter 2: Operational Art in Industrial War

The 20th century saw the gradual evolution of maneuver warfare enabled by the dramatic technological advancement of the period. This allowed for a much more complicated, dynamic, and rapid form of warfare, clearly evident in major combat operations in Iraq in 1991 and 2003. The complicated integration of joint capabilities in sequential and simultaneous operations employed over large battlefields is such a distinct form of warfare that many literary sources claim it is the essence of operational art. The purpose of this chapter is to refute this claim by demonstrating how maneuver warfare is simply a form of operational art and this concept is indeed applicable to other types of wars.

World War I

The ever increasing size of national armies led to massive fronts in the European theater during World War I. Additionally, significant technological developments such as the introduction of the machine gun and artillery led to an overwhelming advantage for opponents occupying defensive positions.[24] Finally, the U.S. conception of depth greatly expanded as the supporting rear and fighting front were now divided by the sea.

Actions at the operational level of war became significantly more difficult during this time period as well. The campaign commander, General Pershing, was initially responsible for developing and executing the campaign plan in support of policy. Additionally, the function of establishing the theater, to include cross continental logistical operations and troop integration was also placed upon his command. The result was the recognition that a single headquarters simply could not establish the theater and simultaneously plan the campaign and supervise tactical action. This led to the partial delegation of campaign planning and execution to a subordinate command. Thus, the function of the operational level of war now rested within two commands. This two command system marks a trend which can be seen clearly throughout U.S. operations for the remainder of the 20th century.

The form of operational art also changed significantly. The enormous size of the armies coupled with the dominance of the defense drove opponents to occupy significant defensive positions in depth and breadth, thus rendering the prospect of a major operation outflanking the

---

[24] Georgii Samoilovich Isserson, *The Evolution of Operational Art* (Translated by Bruce W. Menning. The State Military Publishing House of the USSR People's Defense Commissariat: Moscow, 1937) 19-20.

opponent and striking the enemy rear unlikely.[25] The result was the execution of frontal assaults against well prepared, heavily defended trenches and the loss of millions of soldiers. In this war of attrition, operational art was characterized by the achievement of sequential objectives in a very linear manner and direct manner. The strategic aim simply could not be achieved any other way because of the technological and logistical limitations heavily favored the defense. However, the end of the war saw the introduction of two weapons platforms that would come to dominate warfare for the next century, the airplane and tank.[26] Although not used efficiently during World War I, their introduction during this period highlighted their potential use in future wars. Significant to this period also is how this war led to a period of intense Soviet study which paved the way for the Russian Theory of Deep Operations and the operational concepts within maneuver warfare.

The Russian Theory of Deep Operations

The Russian Deep Operations theory must be addressed not to evaluate its application and effectiveness during World War II, but for the influence this theory had on the United States military in the 1970s and 1980s. The Russian Deep Operations theory was born out of the challenges confronted during World War I and the Russian Civil War which immediately followed. The Soviet analysis of these experiences caused them to question the traditional model of linear tactics used in World War I and study the operational and strategic results achieved during their civil war through deep maneuvers into the opponent's rear areas. This experience was very similar to the methods employed by Grant in the U.S. Civil War. They then rationalized that the ability to outflank an opponent to reach these rear areas would remain improbable as national armies would continue to become more massive and defend the width of their country.

---

[25] Ibid., 30.

[26] Ibid., 10.

They also they recognized that penetrations did occur during the World War I but were not followed by any significant mobile follow on force. Finally, they recognized the new offensive potential of mechanized forces, more viable airpower, and significantly more accurate artillery to break through and exploit the penetration of front line defensive positions to disorganize the enemy in depth.[27]

The Russian cognitive revolution resulted in the development of the Deep Operations theory. Under this new method for conducting war, strategic aims were accomplished by neutralizing the opponent's capability to attain their goals as opposed to destroying their army. This too, parallels Grant's concept of defeating the Confederate army in 1864. However, Russian theory sought to accomplish this aim through the employment of massive army groups to simultaneously attack along the width of the opponent's defensive front with the support of heavy artillery and airpower. This frontal assault would be followed by a penetration at an identified weak point. The penetration force would then separate the front line defenses from the main body. Following the penetration would be an exploitation force which would isolate the main body from its reserves. A final thrust would then be conducted against critical command and control headquarters to ultimately force the collapse of the military system.[28] The theory relied on the concept of operational shock through the depth of the enemy system to force its systemic failure.[29]

The Deep Operations theory reflected a much greater understanding of depth than any previous military had demonstrated. They identified that to conduct sequential deep operations within the theater or multiple theaters would require an unprecedented level of national

---

[27] Ibid., 10

[28] Bruce W. Menning, "Operational Art's Origins" in *Historical Perspectives of the Operational Art* (Washington, D.C: U.S. Army Center for Military History, 2007), 9.

[29] Shimon Naveh, *In Pursuit of Military Excellence: The Evolution of Operational Theory* (London: Routledge, 1997), 211-236.

resources.[30] As such, they broadened their understanding of linking intermediate objectives with strategic requirements and capabilities. The result was a greater emphasis upon the operational level of war to align the selection of intermediate objectives and the strategic aim with the massive sustainment requirements of national industry, critical infrastructure, and mobilization.

The Deep Operations theory had its greatest impact upon U.S. military thought in the area of operational art. Although similar to the German Blitzkrieg in appearance, the Russian theory goes beyond the penetration of enemy front lines to account for the echelonment of forces into a clear, continuous link between the fighting front and supporting rear.[31] Thus, it truly represented an operational concept because it accounted for employment of combined arms and multiple deep strikes to achieve intermediate objectives. The serial accomplishment of intermediate objectives led ultimately to the achievement of the strategic aim. This involved a much broader understanding of time, space, and resources to include the preparation, organization, logistics, engagements, and command arrangements required to achieve the assigned campaign objectives.[32] A final note that must be emphasized is the scale at which this theory was to be employed. The army group commands were executing the major operations under the direction of the Russian staff. Therefore, armies, corps, and divisions were the tactical forces achieving the short term objectives associated with the operational approach. Thus, the army group was the lowest level executing operational art.

World War II

Although the form of operational art was undoubtedly different during World War II, the war did not reveal any critical new developments in the evolution of the concept. The operational level of war did become more complex as the campaign commander was not only directing the

---

[30] Menning, 9.

[31] Naveh, 191-192.

[32] Menning, 9.

joint forces under the command of the United States, but was also integrating other nations into the campaign plan. However, this was evident during World War I as well, although units were employed generally on a national basis.

The form of operational art did change as well, although not to the level envisioned by the Soviet Deep Operations theory. Wider distribution of more reliable radios during the interwar period greatly enhanced the effectiveness of command and control during the Second World War This war also saw advances in the offensive employment of tanks and airplanes.[33] The result was more effective offensive operations and a resurgence of the idea of deep penetrations. However, lack of appropriate logistical capacity generally prevented decisive penetrations as originally intended. Both the Germans and Soviets forces had to conduct many repeating penetrations during the course of the war due to outrunning their logistical support for munitions and fuel. As such, World War II demonstrated how technology and logistics continued to inhibit distributed operations in depth to rapidly force the opponent's collapse.

Operational Art in the United States

In 1975, the United States was recovering from a devastating experience in Vietnam that left the Army a near broken institution.[34] Compounding the problem was the growing threat of a Soviet attack in Europe. General DePuy, the commander of the newly established Training and Doctrine Command (TRADOC), subsequently directed the development of the first Operations Field Manual, FM 101-5 in response to this situation. The manual provided the initial answer to the Soviet threat in the idea of Active Defense.[35] Extremely tactical in nature, active defense focused at the brigade and battalion levels and emphasized their ability to reposition forces

---

[33] Menning p.9

[34] Swain, Richard M. "Filling the Void: The Operational Art and the U.S. Army." In *Operational Art: Developments in the Theory of War*, (Westport, CT: Praeger), 1996, p. 148.

[35] Ibid., 151.

rapidly to combat penetrations. Essentially, it addressed the problem at a tactical level by focusing on the first line defense with little mention of how actions of larger units or other services throughout the operational depth were integrated. This constituted a major problem because the concept of fighting a war of attrition could not work against an opponent with significant advantages in manpower and resources. Thus, the United States faced two significant problems. The first was how to correct the failure in Vietnam of translating tactical success to strategic and political victory. The second was how to fight and win a war on another continent against an opponent with significant advantages in manpower and resources.[36]

The American response to these two problems was the formal recognition of an operational level of war and the articulation and expansion of the theory of operational art. The operational level of war was made explicit in doctrine to codify the function of aligning military action to policy and highlights the importance of combined arms warfare, which stresses the integration of a wide array of forces and capabilities under one common purpose. Combined arms warfare was the method by which the United States would fight outnumbered and win.[37] Finally, this level of war dealt with the reception and support of the diverse forces with significantly different logistical requirements.

The expansion of the theory of operational art and the inclusion of the Soviet concept of operational depth and synchronization drove campaign planners to begin thinking differently about campaign planning. Operational depth referred to space, time, and resources required to strike the enemy throughout the whole of the battlefield.[38] Therefore, campaign commanders began considering the necessary echelonment of forces from one continent to the other while simultaneously transitioning from the defense to the offense in a sequential, synchronized

---

[36] Ibid., 149.

[37] U.S. Department of the Army, FM 100-5, *Operations* (Washington, DC: Government Printing Office, 1986), 25.

[38] Naveh, 301-302.

18

manner. It broadened the concept of a campaign to reflect a more holistic approach, meaning it truly linked the fighting front, tactical actions in Europe, to the supporting rear, the United States industrial base. This took the Active Defense concept and placed it within the operational doctrine of AirLand Battle.

The United States tested these operational concepts within the Air/Land Battle doctrine in the 1991 during the Persian Gulf War. With 360,000 Iraqi forces positioned in Kuwait and just north of the border in Iraq, the U.S. led Coalition deployed to Saudi Arabia to force the withdrawal of Iraq from Kuwait. Through a series of deceptive maneuvers prior to the ground conflict, the coalition was able to force the commitment of additional Iraq troops to into Kuwait. This was followed by a transition to the offense, which employed a large envelopment to the rear and western flank of the Iraqi military thereby preventing its withdrawal. Upon completion of major combat operations, the Coalition had forced the withdrawal of Iraq troops from Kuwait and subsequently destroyed fleeing troops in southern Iraq.[39]

This conflict served to codify the operational concepts adopted by the United States. The method by which the campaign was designed through a continuous discourse between General Schwarzkopf, the campaign commander, General Powell, the military strategist, and President Bush highlighted the important function of the operational level of war.[40] This consisted of a discussion of the objectives and type of war, whether to defend Saudi Arabia or expel the Iraqi military from Kuwait, and the appropriate and eventual revision of troop levels required to ensure rapid strategic success.

General Schwarzkopf demonstrated operational art by gradually refinining the operational approach as tactical action changed the situation. The initial air campaign served as the first step. The subsequent feint in the vicinity of Kuwait City confirmed that Iraqi forces were

---

[39] Brown, 445, 459-464.

[40] Michael R. Gordon and General Bernard E. Trainor, *The Generals' War : The Inside Story of the Conflict in the Gulf* (Boston: Back Bay Books, 1995), 135-40.

fully committed to a static defense. General Schwarzkopf seized this opportunity by then using the air coverage and the feint to reposition the 7th Army to the west, setting conditions for the decisive envelopment. Finally, as overwhelming, and perhaps unexpected, success was achieved in the first few days of the war, the final objective of destroying the Iraq military was modified. This resulted from the strategic discourse of whether to allow the withdrawing Iraqi forces to return to Iraq or continue the attack. The form of operational art, combined arms warfare, demonstrated the unique capabilities of the United States military. It was the result of the complex synchronization of the many services components, coordinated throughout the depth of the theater of operations under one common aim, the destruction of the Republican Guard.

The 3rd Army command and the various service components were also heavily involved in campaign planning. General Schwarzkopf identified the initial intermediate objectives, issued his concept of operations, and allowed the various service components to develop the tactical details of the campaign plan.[41] Of particular note, the corps formations, subordinate to the 7th Army, were the tools of the campaign that executed the tactical objectives outlined by the campaign and major operations. These objectives were tactical in nature, meaning they had definitive, measureable ends. Further, the primary mode of thought at the corps level and below was efficiency and effectiveness with limited thought to the strategic repercussions. Thus, the application of operational art was limited to CENTCOM and the 7th Army commands.

The chapter described the evolution and employment of the two critical operational concepts, operational art and the operational level of war, in the 20th century. Further, it traced the traditional literature on the operational concepts to demonstrate how major combat operations have heavily influenced the United States' modern understanding of these terms. A review of literature available on operational art supports the conclusion that the Persian Gulf War represents what the United States military still views as the epitome of operational art.

---

[41] Swain, *Lucky War*. 90-96, 103-105, 110-131.

Operational Art and War

The major wars of the 20th century demonstrated the necessary functions of the operational level of war. Given the intricate relationships which exist between policy, strategy, and tactical action, the dynamics of a campaign cannot be accommodated without near continuous coordination between the policy maker, military strategist, and campaign commander. In U.S. military history, the collaborations between Grant, Halleck, and Lincoln; Eisenhower, Marshall, and Roosevelt; Schwarzkopf, Powell, and Bush highlight this fact. The next chapter will demonstrate that such discourse was also quite apparent in the preparation for and execution of operations in Iraq in 2003. This discourse is a primary function of the operational level of war and is critical to aligning policy, strategy, and tactics. The requirement for such action still remains valid for any military endeavor to ensure that both the intention of policy is properly understood by the campaign commander and that the policy makers and military strategists understand tactical realities. Additionally, the operational level of war performs the necessary function of integrating and supporting the wide array of forces and capabilities involved in executing a campaign as demonstrated in the 1991 Persian Gulf War. This too, is a necessary and significant component to any war. Therefore, the operational level of war is applicable to counterinsurgency operations.

The major wars of the 20th century also demonstrated the importance of applying operational art to develop campaign plans. The campaign command, or operational level of war, is unique because it is the highest level of military command which controls and directs tactical forces. Therefore, the campaign commander guides the military force towards the achievement of the superior goal for which the war is waged. The 19th and 20th centuries demonstrated this goal, or strategic aim, cannot be achieved in a single battle. Thus, it requires a series of steps to achieve the strategic aim.

The strategic aim must be an abstract concept because what is possible to achieve and exactly what steps the military force will ultimately take to achieve this aim simply cannot be predicted with any certainty at the beginning of the conflict. This is due to the fact that tactical action will reveal new information and create additional challenges which will alter the initial selection of intermediate objectives, methods to achieve those objectives, and potentially the strategic aim itself.

Recognizing this fact, campaign commanders develop a broad operational approach to align the selection of intermediate objectives, and methods to achieve those objectives, with the achievement of the strategic aim. The operational approach also assists commanders with negotiating the cognitive tension that exists between adhering to a higher goal and executing tasks in the most efficient and effective manner possible. Thus, the campaign commander and staff should use operational art in any military endeavor to ensure tactical actions, or intermediate steps, support the attainment of the superior goal. Given that campaign plans are developed at the operational level in Iraq and Afghanistan, the concept of operational art does apply to counterinsurgency operations.

Modern doctrine supports this assertion by stating that operational art is used to plan campaigns and major operations. Where the confusion lies, however, is in who should apply this concept in counterinsurgency operations. Military literature has traditionally studied operational art within the context of the major wars identified in the first two chapters. The purpose of discussing these wars is to demonstrate how in major combat operations operational art is conducted almost exclusively at the operational level of war. Additionally, the campaign achieves the strategic aims in a linear fashion by directing gradual steps to make physical progress towards the destruction or neutralization of the opposing force in this type of war. Each step, or major operation, involves the use of simultaneous or sequential operations to attain intermediate objectives, such as seizing key terrain or destroying enemy formations. Achievement of the intermediate objectives brings the campaign closer to destroying or forcing the collapse of the opposing military force. Therefore, it is a top down process where the campaign controls progress towards achievement of the strategic aim.

Subordinate commands, such as corps in the Napoleonic era and the Persian Gulf War and field armies in the American Civil War and the Russian Deep Operations theory, execute these tactical tasks to support achievement of the intermediate objectives. These assigned tasks have concrete endings, which can be measured. When the tasks are complete, these units are potentially moved to a completely different area and assigned another task with no relation to the previous one. Thus, planning against tactical tasks does not require an operational approach to guide decisions and the selection of tactical actions. Rather, the focus for these tactical units is purely on effectiveness and efficiency. Take, for example, a division tasked with executing a river crossing in major combat operations. The planning associated with this task is complicated and requires creativity, a significant amount of synchronization, and art. However, the difference lies in the idea that this organizations will no longer interact with that specific problem upon completion of its objective. As such, it does not require the application of strategic thought or the cyclical operational art process to consider long term effects of its actions. As such, it lacks the need for an operational approach and the notion of cognitive tension which makes the practice of operational art unique.

The use of tactical planning by corps and divisions size units in major combat operations coupled with the nearly exclusive study of the operational concepts in the context of major combat operations does much to explain the misunderstanding of operational art today. This is clearly evident in the modern doctrinal definition of operational art which states that operational art is used exclusively to plan campaigns and major operations with no mention of its link to achieving strategic aims. The next chapter challenges this definition by describing the different planning processes used by subordinate commands to contend with a much different type of objective in counterinsurgency operations.

Chapter 3: Operational Art in Counterinsurgency Operations

Chapter one defined operational art as the cognitive, cyclical process, using both strategic and tactical thought, to develop and refine an operational approach and select appropriate tactical actions aimed at the simultaneous achievement of intermediate objectives and strategic aims. It further argued that the operational art is applicable to all wars because it is the vital process used to ensure military action is subordinate to and purposeful in achieving the ends of policy and strategic aims. Given that operational art applies to counterinsurgency operations, the purpose of this chapter is to determine who should employ it in counterinsurgency operations.

An analysis of the modern insurgency reveals the unique and highly complex nature of the environment. This complexity has a direct impact on both the strategic aim in counterinsurgency operations and the method used to achieve this aim. The chapter then explores the types of actions conducted by the different command levels to determine who should employ operational art. This analysis is conducted within the context of the second Iraq War to better illustrate these ideas.

The Complex Insurgent Environment

An insurgency is defined as a struggle to control a contested political space between a state, or group of states, and non-state challengers.[42] This struggle is the product of an opportunity to contend for power created from a gradual or dynamic change in the existing social or political system. The United States military intervention in Iraq in 2003 serves as a clear example of creating this opportunity by inflicting a dynamic shock in the social system by disbanding the government, military, and law enforcement institutions following the collapse of the Saddam Hussein regime.[43] The lack of institutional support and security organizations

---

[42] David Kilcullen, "Counter-insurgency Redux," *Survival 48, no. 4* (Winter 2006-2007), 2.

[43] Linda Robinson, *Tell Me How This Ends: General David Petraeus and the Search for a Way Out of Iraq* (New York: Public Affairs, 2008), 3.

provided a level of uncertainty among the members of the society which manifested itself in the form of fear. That fear and uncertainty create opportunity which is subsequently exploited through the use of violence and coercion, a situation that characterizes much of the environment in Iraq.

In addition to fear, other deep rooted social, economic, religious, and political issues may also be exploited. Recent history has demonstrated that countries with severe economic hardship and histories of social inequalities are more susceptible to unstable environments and revolution.[44] Specific to Iraq, decades of social repression through exclusive rule and state intervention in economics resulting in the unequal distribution of wealth played a significant factor in mobilizing certain portions of the population. The Shia majority had been marginalized under Saddam Hussein by limiting education, job opportunities, and positions in the government. The Sunni minority, on the other hand, enjoyed complete dominance in the government and better access and placement in education and jobs, while also retaining a much higher standard of living.[45]

The opportunity created by national, regional, or local shock, combined with fear and the effects of decades of social, economic, and political inequality gave rise to a wide range of actors in the environment, the primary of which were insurgents. The purpose of insurgencies varies widely throughout history from fighting to replace the existing government, to fragmenting the country, or simply paralyzing the society to facilitate a higher purpose not associated with the specific country.[46] Iraq presents a unique challenge in that the insurgency presented a number of major groups with vastly different interests. Al Qaida's aim was to exhaust the United States

---

[44] Misagh Parsa, *States, Ideologies, and Social Revolutions* (Cambridge, UK: Cambridge University Press, 200), 19-25.

[45] Heather S. Gregg, Hy S. Rothstein and John Arquilla, eds., *The Three Circles of War: Understanding the Dynamics of Conflict in Iraq* (Washington, D.C.: Potomac Books Inc., 2010), 12-16.

[46] Kilcullen, "Counter-insurgency Redux," 3.

economically and politically by fostering a chaotic environment in Iraq. This objective focused on paralyzing the government by attacking Coalition Forces, the Iraqi government, and the Shia population.[47] Sunni nationalist insurgent groups, such as the 1920th Revolutionary Brigade, sought to challenge the government to regain a dominant position in Iraqi society.[48] Shia Extremists, heavily influenced by Iran, sought to paralyze the government, much like Al Qaida, to create an opportunity for Iranian intervention and influence.[49] The Jaysh Al Mahdi, a Shia nationalist group, projected force against nearly ever military actor in the country to ultimately achieve a more dominant position of influence inside the government.[50]

An important distinction is that the four insurgent groups are merely the military action arm of political actors or groups either inside the country or abroad. Further, these actors control various information, religious, and social organizations to achieve their purpose as well. Although this description is an oversimplification because certainly more groups exist in Iraq, it serves to highlight the powerful organizations with vastly different capabilities and significantly different agendas contending for power and influence. It also demonstrates how the military must contend with the underlying causes, perceptions, and the many different insurgent groups.[51]

The purpose of defining the numerous actors, groups, and pre-existing social conditions is first to demonstrate the level of complexity that exists in dealing with what is essentially a social problem in counterinsurgency.[52] To better understand complexity, the different groups interacting in this environment will be described each as separate systems. These systems range

---

[47] Loretta Napoleoni, *Insurgent Iraq: Al-Zarqawi and the New Generation* (New York: Seven Stories Press, 2005), 188-93.

[48] Thomas R. Mockaitis, *Iraq and the Challenge of Counterinsurgency* (Westport: Praeger, 2008), 109.

[49] David Kilcullen, *The Accidental Guerrilla: Fighting Small Wars in the Midst of a Big One* (Oxford: Oxford University Press, USA, 2009), 126.

[50] Robinson, 161-63.

[51] Mockaitis, 19.

[52] Gregg, 117

from military units, insurgent groups, political entities, and so forth. Complexity theory describes how systems are composed of a significant number of parts. Additionally, these parts are interdependent, meaning they interact continuously with one another. Because they are interdependent, a change in one part will have second and third order effects throughout the entire system potentially creating new problems or revealing previously undetected ones.[53] Further, the systems themselves are interdependent because they exist in the same environment. Therefore, a change in one part of a single system has second and third order effects throughout the other systems in the environment as well.[54] This means that the many different groups, whether it be insurgent, police, or the population segments, all interact and thus influence each other and the environment in unpredictable ways.

The Effects of Complexity on the Strategic Aim

The complexity of the insurgent environment highlights a potential change in the focus of U.S. counterinsurgency operations. Although the counterinsurgent is by definition the host nation government, the United States is nevertheless heavily involved in assisting those governments. Thus, the United States is another counterinsurgent organization. However, its agenda is different from that of the host nation government. For the United States, the task is not to defeat all the various insurgencies. The accomplishment of such a task in the limited amount of time available given the significant resource requirement and the influence of public opinion is highly improbable. Rather, as Dr. David Kilcullen argues, the objective is to impose order on an unstable and chaotic environment to facilitate a withdrawal on favorable terms.[55] A level of stability provides the base from which the host nation can gradually improve conditions and eventually

---

[53] U.S. Department of the Army, FM 3-24, *Counterinsurgency* (Washington, DC: Headquarters, Department of the Army, 2006), 4-1.

[54] Antoine J. Bousquet, *The Scientific Way of Warfare: Order and Chaos on the Battlefields of Modernity* (New York: Columbia University Press, 2009), 175.

[55] David Kilcullen, "Counter-insurgency Redux, ", 10.

remove the majority of the threats without significant external assistance. Evidence of this shift in the military aim is clearly articulated in the revised Iraq campaign plan of 2007.[56]

The strategic aim of stability thus marks a clear shift in the use of military and national power. During major combat operations, physical attainment of objectives with definitive ends dominates military planning at most echelons. However, the objective now changes from a measureable one that can be seized, destroyed, or secured to an objective that is qualitative and subjective. More importantly, it is a condition that must be gained and maintained, highly variant and prone to assured fluctuation based on action within this complex environment. However, the higher driving concept is to gain and maintain a reasonable level of stability to foster political maneuver and ultimately withdrawal.[57] Thus, the military transitions from a problem with definitive, measurable ends to one that is qualitative, constantly fluctuating, and without an identified ending. Therefore, the aim is very much abstract and conceptual in nature.

The Effects of Complexity on Achieving the Strategic Aim

As described earlier, the complexity at the campaign level is significant when factoring in all the different problems, political and insurgent groups, diverse population demographics, and military units that exist throughout the nation. There are simply too many systems that constantly interact across the entire country for campaign planners to fully understand. Without such an understanding, precise actions and their consequences cannot properly be assessed or determined at that level.

As such, the military force employs a decentralized approach to manage this complexity more effectively. Units are assigned areas of operations to match force capabilities proportionate to the complexity and uniqueness of these local areas. This essentially breaks down a highly

---

[56] Thomas E. Ricks, *The Gamble: General David Petraeus and the American Military Adventure in Iraq, 2006-2008*, 1St Edition ed. (New York: Penguin Press HC, The, 2009), 155.

[57] Ibid., 164.

28

complex and large environment into manageable, smaller pieces. It also allows the military force to focus effort against the problems unique to each of the local areas. For example, each major city in Iraq hosted members of each of the insurgent groups along with the general problems that exist throughout the country. However, the proportion of the different groups and extent of the problems vary from area to area. This trend is true at all levels, whether it be village, district, city, or region. Thus, the decentralized approach allows for tailored solutions to the unique problems that exist in the different local areas. More importantly, it highlights the unique way the strategic aim is achieved in counterinsurgency. Rather than being top down, the complexity and diverse situations in the local areas force the process to be bottom up. Said another way, national stability is the product of local stability. As such, the strategic aim, stability, is shared by subordinate commands in permanently assigned areas of operations.

The remaining section of the chapter explores the planning and activities conducted by the major commands in a decentralized counterinsurgency environment. For simplicity, the various command groups are described in three categories consistent with the general functions each performs. The first is that of the campaign command. In Iraq, this is Multi National Force – Iraq (MNF-I) and Multi National Corps – Iraq (MNC-I). The second group discussed is the major commands. These are the commands that act between the campaign command, or operational level of war, and the lowest level of command that is assigned an area of operation. In Iraq, these are the divisions, brigades, and battalions. The junior commands, the final group discussed, are the lowest level of command assigned a permanent area of operation. In Iraq, these are generally the company commands.

Campaign Commands in Counterinsurgency

The changes of command in 2006 and 2007 of the Multi National Force – Iraq (MNF-I) and Multi National Corps – Iraq (MNC-I) led to the development of a new campaign plan which reflect not only the function of the operational level of war, but also the application of operational art. The MNF-I and MNC-I structure was established in 2004 to deal with the increased demands of operating between the strategic and political authorities of the United States and managing the tactical execution of assigned forces within the theater. Major General Petraeus assumed command of MNF-I early in 2007 and his actions reflect the activities of a commander performing at the operational level of war. He was heavily involved in not only understanding strategic and political intent, but was influential in the development of the Iraq counterinsurgency strategy. The end product of this discourse was identification of stability as the new strategic aim.[58] Additionally, his continuous testimonies to Congress assisted in balancing ends and means by successfully lobbying for the 30,000 soldier increase while simultaneously influencing the American public opinion to sustain the war.[59]

Major General Petraeus was also heavily involved in discourse with the MNC-I commander, General Odierno, who assumed command in late 2006. The MNC-I commander, in turn, focused heavily on translating the strategic aim into an operational approach and a new campaign plan.[60] This campaign plan provided an overall logic and method of employing military units to achieve this endstate. Further, it reorganized the assigned areas of operation and the apportionment of forces to set conditions for units to be successful in the conduct of operations.

Further analysis of the MNC-I campaign plan reveals that it lacked detail in prescribing tactical action in the form of major operations and intermediate objectives. This is very different than in major combat operations. Rather, it provided subordinate commands with two broad concepts to solve problems within their assigned areas of operation. The first is the unifying theme, or operational approach, which begins the process of translating strategic aims into tactical

---

[58] Ibid., 155, 164.

[59] Ricks, 223.

[60] Ibid., 165, 201.

30

action by providing "logical" lines of operations. These lines of operation are an expression of commander's vision and describe the key methods by which the force will achieve the end state.[61] The second is the general offensive concept of "Clear-Hold-Build". This is a conceptual model that was to be executed similarly by all commands within their assigned areas of operation.

The lack of detail in a counterinsurgency campaign plan occurs for a number of reasons. The first is due to the idea of local relevance, included in the Army Counterinsurgency Manual FM 3-24. Local relevance states that each area is unique due to complexity and thus requires modified approaches to achieve effective action throughout the depth of the operational environment.[62] As such, a campaign plan issued at the theater level in counterinsurgency operations serves its purpose by providing general direction to subordinate commands but falls short in translating strategy to tactical action because of the unique circumstances and dynamic nature of the local environments.

Given that each local area is different, the campaign recognizes that stability may not be achieved sequentially or in a planned, orderly, and predictable process. Rather, stability on a mass scale is the product of stability in each unique area. Thus, local actions to achieve stability should mirror national actions on a much smaller scale and should generally have the same purpose. This is a fundamental change from executing major combat operations where the purpose of all actions is to support a main effort, who in turn accomplishes the higher command's mission. In a counterinsurgency environment, gaining stability on a mass scale requires simultaneous operations across a large number of unique local areas, each contributing equally, but in potentially unique ways, to achieving national stability. More importantly, the military problem at the local level now mirrors that of the national level in that it is unending and constantly fluctuating. As such, military operations tend to be decentralized in this environment and

---

[61] U.S. Department of the Army, FM 3-24, (2006),.4-4 to 4-5.

[62] Ibid., 4-4 to 4-5.

subordinate commands must contend with an aim of stability as the campaign does, in a smaller form.

Major Commands in Counterinsurgency

Major commands, such as divisions, brigades, and battalions in Iraq, are also charged with the aim of achieving stability within their assigned area of operation. Because stability itself is an abstract aim, a process must be used to first understand the complexity within their specific environment and tailor a series of general actions to achieve this abstract aim. Similar to the campaign level, achieving this aim requires a long range planning process to guide the conduct of tactical action and refine objectives, restrictions, and methods within their unique area of operation. This is accomplished by using the existing design framework and lines of operation, provided by the campaign plan, to further tailor an operational approach specific to their assigned area of operations.[63] Also similar to the campaign level, major commands refrain from directing an overwhelming sequence of specific tactical actions to subordinates. This too is the result of complexity at the lower levels as the major commands lack detailed knowledge of the localities within its boundaries to precisely direct action within specific areas.[64] As such, major commands exercise only limited control over the forces. They use their operational approach, and commander's intent to direct action to affect decisive portions of their area of operation and to communicate to their subordinate commands.

Given that major commands exercise only limited control over tactical forces, their focus is on shaping and synchronizing actions within their assigned area of operations. They accomplish this in two ways. First, they direct specific operations of varying scale in response to opportunity or the need to create opportunity in their assigned area. This can involve the massing

---

[63] Ibid., 4-5

[64] Ibid., A-8.

of units to temporary areas of operation or tasking units to support a larger operation by executing specific tasks within their area of operation. An example of this was the major operation that occurred within Baghdad against the various Shia insurgent groups. This operation led to multiple companies massing in Shia safe havens throughout various areas of northern and western Baghdad while combined operations took place in Sadr City with multiple U.S. battalions and Iraqi divisions.[65] Upon completion of the division level major operation, those battalions and companies returned to their previously assigned areas of operations. Significant to note is that the subordinate units tasked with executing a major operation in this instance are simply the tools of the higher command directing the operation. Thus, these units are executing traditional tactical planning against short term missions with definitive, measurable ends. Thus, only the major command is employing operational art in this instance.

The second method by which major commands affect their assigned area of operations is by directing the subordinate command to execute specific action that will achieve an effect throughout the higher commands area of operation. These particular tasks include lethal strikes, raids, economic, political, or other non-military activities. Such action is directed at those things that specifically enhance the command's position within the area of operation and along the lines of operation.

LTC Dale Kuehl served as a battalion commander in Ademeyia, Baghdad from 2006 through 2008. Featured in Thomas Rick's book "The Gamble," LTC Kuehl provided an extensive interview which details the process by which his unit planned and executed operations. What he describes is precisely the application of operational art. He first identifies how COL J.R. Burton, the brigade commander charged with stabilizing northwest Baghdad in 2006, provided a broad vision in the form of a campaign plan nested within the MNC-I and MND-B plans. LTC

---

[65] Marisa Cochrane, *Special Groups Regenerate: Iraq Report 11*, in the The Institute For The Study Of War, http://www.understandingwar.org/operation/operation-peace (accessed March 21, 2011).

33

Kuehl then developed a battalion level campaign plan that consisted of five lines of operation, which identified critical objectives the battalion was to achieve through tactical action. Further, he refined these lines of operation periodically as the unit conducted operations and refined their understanding of the changing conditions. Of particular note, the rise of the Sons of Iraq significantly altered the strategic picture within this area of operations. Finally, he identified how each iteration became more precise and effective in directing tactical action and forcing positive change.[66] This describes the essence of operational art.

Junior Commands in Counterinsurgency

A final method by which the campaign and major commands accomplish their purpose is by allowing the junior commands assigned an area of operations the ability to pursue stability in their local area using mission command. In Iraq, these are generally company commands. Unique to these commands is the burden of action when orders from higher headquarters no longer prescribe specific action. FM 3-24 identifies action taken in these instances as commander's initiative and describes it as the assumption of independent responsibility for deciding and initiating independent actions when the concept of operations or orders no longer apply or when an unanticipated opportunity leading to accomplishment of the commander's intent presents itself.[67] Because of the uniqueness and complexity of each local area, these commanders execute this independent initiative on a continuous basis. Thus, they consistently develop and prescribe tactical action that they best feel will achieve stability within their local area.

Nested within the refined operational approaches of the various subcommands, the junior commands, design an operational approach and execute smaller operations to shape their assigned area of operations. Unlike the major commands, however, they direct specific tactical actions

---

[66] Dale Kuehl, "Inside the Surge: 1-5 Cavalry in Ameriyah", *Small Wars Journal* (14 March 2011): 3, http://smallwarsjournal.com (accessed March 21, 2011).

[67] U.S. Department of the Army, FM 3-24, *Counterinsurgency* (2006), 4-4

daily to their assigned units. The tools these company commands use are the platoons. Much like larger units in major combat operations, these platoons serve as the action arm to accomplish tactical tasks as directed by the company commander.

Critical to this examination is the strategic mode of thought required of the junior commands. Specifically, the junior commander must account for the second and third order effects of the use of force. The idea of restraint and discrimination are critical factors for junior commanders in this environment. For example, insurgents, as part of their plan to gain or maintain the initiative, will often attempt to provoke the opponent into over reacting. IED strikes in Iraq serve this purpose. Following a strike, the junior commander has the option to conduct an immediate offensive action, such as a cordon and search. However, that company commander has another option in doing nothing given that intelligence may be minimal and the situation not clearly understood. This common situation highlights the cognitive tension that exists between strategic aims and tactical objectives. Tactical thinking would sway the commander immediately conduct a large operation to seize the insurgents, thereby taking action at the very least and maintaining the morale of the unit. However, the second and third order effects of conducting this operation without intelligence and high levels of emotion may not be advantageous to achievement of the higher purpose, the strategic aim of stability. Strategic thinking, on the other hand, would sway the commander to analyze second and third order effects of potential actions to determine which action best contributes to the achievement of the strategic aim as opposed to the tactical desire to take action. The application of strategic thinking may inform the commander to first develop the necessary intelligence, and strike precisely at a later time against the specific threat, thereby avoiding unnecessary adverse reactions against the population. This is a prime example of cognitive tension and highlights the unique mode of thought required of subordinate commands in counterinsurgency operations.

The requirements in counterinsurgency operations to direct and coordinate numerous political, economic, and social activities also present a tremendous challenge for the junior commander. Again, it is here that discretion and judgment play a vital role as second and third order effects which must be analyzed to determine the most stabilizing activities. Further, these actions must be synchronized and analyzed within the context of the complex environment. Determining which politicians to empower, which economic opportunities to pursue, and which social issues to address becomes a major analytic process involving consideration of second and third order effects as well. This is much more daunting a task than one would think at first sight. For example, choosing a politician to work with publicly entails a wide range of second and third order effects. This politician may have hidden or alternate agendas. The population may know his agenda but it may not be clear to the commander. As such, working with that individual sends a message to the population implicitly which may serve to enhance cooperation and confidence among the population or deter it.[68] Further, an alternate agenda could inhibit economic progress while empowering insurgent groups. Thus, the junior commander employs an iterative approach where he empowers the leader, then waits to identify the results before making further decisions. Contending with multiple political representatives and their agendas remains a common occurrence in the counterinsurgency environment and further complicates the junior commander's determination of what actions will put their organizations in the most advantageous positions.

The nature of the problem assigned to junior commands in this environment highlights the need for the development of a long term plan, or operational approach, to guide their decision making and tactical actions. Further, the operational approach requires constant reassessment as actions change the local situation and reveal new or previously unforeseen information. Thus, this iterative process of aligning their strategic aim, local stability, with the selection and methods for

---

[68] Mockaitis, 131.

achieving their intermediate objectives, highlights the application of operational art at the junior command level.

Operational Art in Counterinsurgency

The aim in modern counterinsurgency operations is to gain an appropriate level of stability to facilitate political maneuver and eventual military withdrawal on favorable terms. To achieve stability the military must contend with not just the insurgent groups, but also the underlying social, economic, and political problems plaguing the society. Because of the very dynamic and complex environment, regions and local jurisdictions must be apportioned to subordinate commands in order to address the unique challenges each local area presents. Therefore, stability at a national level is generally a product of local stability. This means that a major part of the strategic aim is accomplished within these local areas. Stability across the local areas leads to stability at the national level. Thus, each subordinate command assigned an area of operation is ultimately contending with achieving part of the strategic aim.

Because all commands are attempting to simultaneously achieve stability, the planning and operations process is generally similar between these different commands. All commands must develop an operational approach to tailor solutions to their unique local areas. This operational approach then guides the decisions on tactical action and the use of force. Additionally, these commands must continuously refine their operational approach and intermediate objectives as tactical action reveals new information. Also, all commands shape the environment within their assigned areas of operation with the provided assets. Finally, all commands direct tactical action to various subunits to seize or maintain the initiative within their assigned area of operation. The junior commander, however, is unique because the burden of action ultimately falls on them when the higher order is no longer sufficient to direct tactical action. Thus, junior commands practice operational art when attempting to achieve stability within their local areas.

The application of operational art is inherent in attempting to achieve strategic aims using military force. Thus, inherent in counterinsurgency operations is the conduct of operational art across multiple echelons down to the lowest command owning a permanently assigned area of operation. This is operational art because these commands lie in the middle of the spectrum of the cognitive tension. One the one hand, commanders charged with stability must achieve tactical victory. This is necessary to keep their soldiers alive, maintain unit morale, and create and seize opportunities. On the other hand, however, is the need to think strategically to align tactical actions with the long term aim of stability. This ensures that action is purposeful in contributing to the overall aim. This tension exists at all levels of command assigned a permanent area of operations in counterinsurgency.

Chapter 4: Implications

The monograph has argued that operational art has both a strategic and a tactical aspect which makes it unique from other forms of planning. Further, it is the cognitive tension and use of an operational approach to deal with both abstract aims and tactical requirements which defines it. Because the campaign relies on local stability to achieve national stability, it provides only a focus and general concept for the achievement of stability in the local areas. Therefore, stability is the aim of subordinate commands as well. Subordinate commands practice operational art to achieve this aim. This chapter focuses on how well the Army addresses this issue and considers the implications for current Army doctrine, the Army education system, and the conduct of future counterinsurgency operations.

Doctrine

The use of operational art by subordinate commands in the counterinsurgency environment has three primary implications with respect to doctrine. The first is a clear need to refine the definition of operational art to accurately reflect the significance of this process. The second is to divorce operational art from the operational level of war to gain an appreciation for its application along the entire spectrum of conflict. The final aspect which must be addressed is the elaboration of the idea of local relevance from FM 3-24 which does much to prove that subordinate commands are applying operational art in counterinsurgency operations.

U.S. Army Field Manual 3-0

Doctrinal definitions are important because they provide the foundation, or common language, for learning and discussion. Unfortunately, the current definition of operational art must change to better describe the concept and its applicability to counterinsurgency. The first definition of operational art in the United States military appeared in the 1986 Army Field Manual FM 100-5: "the employment of military forces to attain strategic goals in a theater of war or theater of operations, through the design, organization, and conduct of campaigns and major operations."[69] There are two key aspects of this definition. The first is the explicit link of strategic aims to tactical actions. The second is the linking of operational art to campaigns and major operations. This second part is a clear reflection of the context in which it was created. In 1986, the Army was heavily focused on major combat operations. In this type of war, the campaign plan determines the physical objectives to be seized while the larger units execute these objectives in major combat operations. These objectives have definitive, measureable ends which require little thought to the second and third order effects of action taken. Upon completion of these tasks, that same unit is picked up and moved to do another task in support of the campaign plan. Therefore, operational art was exclusive to campaign planners, or the operational level of war, given the type of war the U.S. military was preparing to fight.

Unfortunately, the present definition does little to address the changing context and experience the military has gained over the last ten years of conducting counterinsurgency operations. The most recent Army Field Manual 3-0 dated April 2008 defines it as "the

---

[69] Swain, "Filling the Void: The Operational Art and the U.S. Army." 165.

application of creative imagination by commanders and staffs-supported by their skill, knowledge, and experience-to design strategies, campaigns, and major operations and organize and employ military forces.[70] This definition reflects a clear lack of understanding of this concept as it fails to identify operational art as linking military action to strategic aims, the most unique and important aspect of operational art. Rather, it blindly states that operational art is used to develop strategies, campaigns, and major operations, a statement which reflects the context of major combat operations.

The significance is that the current definition of operational art simply lacks any substance. This severely inhibits understanding of what makes this concept distinct from tactical planning. Rather than focusing on who uses operational art, such as those who plan campaigns and major operations, the definition should focus on the essence of the concept. Operational art is a cognitive process of continuous interpretation and refinement of intermediate objectives to ultimately achieve a strategic aim. An accurate definition is a clear starting point for the study of any concept. Without this definition, the understanding and evolution of this concept will be difficult at best.

The second major issue with operational art is the traditional coupling of operational art with the operational level of war. The operational level of war was originally defined in 1986 as the command that planned and oversaw the campaign.[71] Those that planned and oversaw major operations were considered part of the operational level of war because they were decisive components of the campaign in AirLand Battle.[72] The elements of operational design were those

---

[70] U.S. Department of the Army, FM 3-0, *Operations* (Washington, DC: Headquarters, Department of the Army, 2008), 3-1

[71] U.S. Department of the Army, FM 100-5, *Operations* (Washington, DC: Government Printing Office, 1982), 2-3.

[72] U.S. Department of the Army, FM 100-5, *Operations* (1986), 31.

key concepts central to the development of a campaign plan.[73] Operational maneuver was a large maneuver that placed the campaign command in a decisive position of advantage to achieve its objectives.[74] Finally, operational art was the intellectual process by which the campaign plan was developed.[75] Simply said, the adjective "operational" described those things that applied to the campaign.

Operations over the last ten years have revealed that certain aspects previously thought to be exclusive to the campaign level are in fact applicable to tactical units as well. Examples include the elements of operational design and the idea of an operational approach.[76] Areas of operation are now commonly referred to as the operational environment as well. What is clear is that the term "operational" no longer describes the campaign. Therefore, the term simply has no meaning at all until better defined in doctrine.

The easiest fix to this situation would be to define operational as those things that apply to the planning of operations. In turn, the Army would have to define the term "operation", which surprisingly, is currently absent from Army doctrine. A potential definition is a series of missions executed to achieve an intermediate objective along an operational approach. Likewise, the operational level of war should be changed to the intermediate level of war to avoid linking terms to levels of war.

U.S. Army Field Manual 3-24 Counterinsurgency

Also emphasized in the monograph is the idea of local relevance identified in the Army's Counterinsurgency Field Manual 3-24. Although the aim of this manual is to assist senior

---

[73] Ibid., 179.

[74] Ibid., 12.

[75] Ibid., 10

[76] U.S. Department of the Army, FM 3-0, *Operations* (2008), 3-1 and U.S. Department of the Army, FM 5-0, *The Operations Process* (Washington, DC: Headquarters, Department of the Army, 2008), 3-6.

commanders and staff in developing campaign plans for counterinsurgency, it does identify one critical concept that has the potential to shape and foster new ideas on how the military views tactical planning in counterinsurgency. This is the idea of local relevance discussed earlier in Chapter 2. Local relevance refers to the understanding that the general problems in each local area are similar to the larger whole, or theater, but are also quite unique in its specific problems.[77] This means that each area requires a unique approach and certainly different tactical actions.

FM 3-24 must elaborate on the significance of local relevance. This concept has a number of key implications. The first is the recognition that the campaign plan may not be by itself wholly sufficient in translating the strategic aim to tactical action. Second, this implies that the same process must then be conducted at lower echelons to continue to translate the aim into tactical action. Third, the theater or campaign commander must provide guidance to properly orient subordinate commanders in their strategic thought. An example of this is General Petraeus' guidance to local commander for the conduct of counterinsurgency.[78] This document essentially laid out how commanders should think strategically when operating inside their area of operations. Finally, it implies that the strategic aim is not solely the purview of the campaign commander. The strategic aim may be directly what the subordinate commanders are planning against when developing tactical action.

Education

The monograph argues that the application of operational art is critical to the success of subordinate commands in counterinsurgency operations. Therefore, this subject must be incorporated into all officers schooling beginning with the Captain's Career Course. The Army

---

[77] U.S. Department of the Army, FM 3-24, *Counterinsurgency* (2006), 4-5

[78] Ricks, p. 369-371

methodology is a practical solution to partially meet this need. The design process is used for ill structured problems to help commander and staff gain a deeper understanding of the military problems and the many dynamic factors that affect the problem.[79] Although design is not a requirement for the conduct of operational art, the design process does assist in building an operational approach.[80] The operational approach is a critical aspect of operational art because it represents strategic thought applied to the development of intermediate objectives which leads to achievement of a higher purpose. Both the infantry captain's career course and ILE provide an excellent opportunity to teach this process and will give both company and battalion commanders more tools to accomplish their assigned objectives and aims in counterinsurgency operations.

Operations

Modern counterinsurgency operations in Iraq and Afghanistan demonstrated a marked shift in the employment of the military force by permanently assigning areas of operations to lower echelons of command such as battalions and companies. Cleary the success of these decentralized operations combined with units occupying combat outposts in their assigned areas of operation proved a remarkable success Iraq from 2007-2009. However, the application of operational art by subordinate commands has a few significant drawbacks which must be clearly understood to properly evaluate when and where to accept risk in the form of organizing and fighting a counterinsurgency campaign.

The first area of concern is the tremendous burden placed on the junior commands permanently assigned an area of operations. When an area of operations is assigned to a company in counterinsurgency operations, the company commander becomes the central figure in the flow of information. However, a company commander does not have the appropriate staff to facilitate

---

[79] U.S. Department of the Army, FM 5-0, *The Operations Process* (2010), 3-5.
[80] Ibid., 3-11.

43

decision making and serve as a hub of information. Even if the company staff became more robust, there is little guarantee that a captain can oversee and direct this staff appropriately, while constantly developing, executing, and assessing tactical plans that contribute to the overall aim. Of greatest importance however, is the potential for company commanders to lose sight of the tactical aspect of conducting operations. Developing and refining operational approaches can come to dominate the company commander's mind. However, the other aspect of operational art calls for the efficient and effective application of tactics to achieve intermediate objectives. At the campaign level, this aspect is delegated to the next subordinate command. Company commanders, however, have no subordinate commands below them, nor any officers with extensive tactical experience. As such, company commanders must remain cognizant of the need to spend a significant amount of time on tactics to protect and preserve the force.

Another major concern with decentralization is that of synchronizing the application of operational art. As discussed in the previous chapter, the lowest unit assigned an area of operations is charged with stabilizing the area. Thus, it must employ a complex problem solving process that utilizes strategic thinking to determine tactical actions that produce and maintain this condition. However, junior commands can affect city, regional, or even national objectives through their many local decisions. As such, they generally lack the intimate knowledge of the city and regional conditions to determine how their actions affect conditions outside their area of operation. In theory, then, multiple commanders applying operational art within the same chain of command can essentially be working against each other because of the interdependent nature of systems across unit boundaries. This is not so much a concern when trying to increase the level of security as military units within the chain of command generally have a wide range of access to enemy information and intelligence. However, when the pressing issues move beyond security to economic and political initiatives, this becomes a greater concern because of the lack of knowledge by company commanders.

The final issue with decentralization is that it greatly reduces flexibility of the force across the depth of the operational environment. Once a company is physically moved to an outpost, it is now tied to the local terrain. The ability of a higher level command to utilize those forces to meet major challenges across a larger area is now severely degraded. No longer do the higher level commands have the option of directing patrolling or focusing a significant amount of combat power in one general location for a sustained period of time. Rather, this approach implicitly states that each local area is as important as the next, all contributing equally to the military aim, thus requiring equal distribution of force. At some point, it must be recognized that certain areas are capable of self regulation and more force may be apportioned disproportionately to other area of more immediate concern.

The purpose of this section is to highlight the inefficiencies and challenges with subordinate organizations performing operational art. Commanders and staffs must be cognizant of these drawbacks to better assess progress and facilitate decision making. The potential to centralize decision making and operations should increase as the dominant issues move beyond security to the political and economic realms.

Conclusion

The rise of national armies, the industrial revolution, and the increased lethality of firearms changed the character of war significantly in the mid 1800s. The vast increase in manpower and resources required to fight and sustain a war eventually led to the separation of political leadership from the employment of military forces. This period also saw the equipping and movement of massive armies while forcing the dispersion of these armies on the battlefield into a vast number of formations and numerous battles. In addition to eliminating the possibility of destroying the opposing Army, no longer could a single military commander directly control the tactical engagements or battles inside the theater of war.[81]

These challenges forced an evolutionary process in the structure of war planning reflected in the operational concepts. These concepts addressed the gap between the political and military leaders by bridging political purpose and military action. Further, these concepts defined how the senior military commander, absent from most battles, develops a broad plan for tactical actions within the theater by determining when and where to give battle and for what purpose. Finally, they addressed the challenge of not being able to destroy an opposing force by utilizing a creative process of employing the force in any way possible to set conditions for successive operations to dislocate the opposing Army or force its capitulation.

These concepts were first made explicit and closely studied by the Soviet Union following the disaster of World War I. Coined the operational level of war and operational art, they described the structure of campaign planning and the intellectual process required to link military forces from the industrial base to the front line, while employing them in successive operations designed to penetrate deep into the enemy system to force its collapse.[82] These concepts were then adopted by the United States in 1986 following the strategic failure in Vietnam and described the intellectual process that underpinned campaign planning in the AirLand Battle doctrine.[83]

What makes operational art unique to tactical planning lies in the type of problem the command is attempting to solve. Operational artists deal with abstract, strategic aims which require the development of an operational approach to guide intermediate actions. Tactical planning, on the other hand, addresses short term problems with definitive, measurable ends.

---

[81] Menning, p.4-6

[82] Menning, 9.

[83] Brown, 439-440.

Because strategic aims are long term military goals that support national policy, the application of operational art requires both strategic and tactical thinking. Strategic thinking is used to determine what objectives, when met, will bring about the achievement of this aim. This involves a thorough understanding of complexity within the environment to better weigh the second and third order effects of potential actions and select those most beneficial to achieving the strategic aim. It also involves tactical thinking to determine how those objectives can be met in the most effective and efficient manner possible given the strategic constraints.

The strategic and tactical requirements together create a cognitive tension that exists within commands charged with achieving a strategic aim. This tension describes the potential conflict between what is required to achieve the higher objective and what is required to bring the immediate situation to an end as soon as possible.[84] Thus, the critical aspect of accepting short term losses or inefficiencies to achieve a higher purpose is very much unique to this higher mode of thought and clearly separates tactical planning from operational art.

This mode of thought is generally unique to those commands that are decisive elements of the campaign in major combat operations. However, in counterinsurgency operations, the strategic aim of stability cannot be achieved by a top down approach because of the increased complexity that exists when dealing with this social problem. As such, areas are proportioned to subordinate commands to better grasp the complexity of each of the local areas and tailor specific solutions to these local areas.[85] Each of the subordinate commands achieve part of the strategic aim, stability, within their assigned area of operations. Thus, the subordinate commands charged with stability, employ operational art by developing an operational approach to determine intermediate objectives and select, sequence, and synchronize action to simultaneously achieve intermediate objectives and progress towards the strategic aim.

---

[84] Naveh, 13.

[85] U.S. Department of the Army, FM 3-24, *Counterinsurgency* (2006), 4-5

47

What is important to gather from the study of operational art is that the military must recognize that its description is inadequate and unhelpful to the common reader. Filled with contradicting thoughts and synonymous use of different terms, the military must first determine if it wishes to accept this concept as the art of planning campaigns or continue to develop the concept through study and a deeper understanding. Either way, doctrine must be written more precisely to better communicate the concept of operational art and therefore better assist those junior commands in applying this concept.

This dilemma must be addressed in the formal education systems across the Army as well. The Army design methodology, although not required to conduct operational art, does offer some immediate benefits in addressing this challenge. It assists commanders in understanding the complexity in their environment and tailoring a long term solution to the problems with which they are confronted. Lastly, commanders at all levels should be cognizant of the drawbacks of employing operational art at multiple levels. Operational art has the potential to overwhelm subordinate commands at the expense of sound tactics, which is ultimately responsible for keeping soldiers alive.

Bibliography

Celeski, John D. *Operationalizing COIN*, Florida: The JSOU Press, 2005.

Clausewitz, Carl Von. *On War*. Princeton: Princeton University Press, 1984.

Cochrane, Marissa. "Special Groups Regenerate: Iraq Report 11." *The Institute For The Study Of War*. http://www.understandingwar.org/

Dolman, Everett. *Pure Strategy: Power and Policy in the Space and Information Age (Strategy and History)*. New ed. New York: Routledge, 2005.

Isserson, Georgii Samoilovich. *The Evolution of Operational Art* translated by Bruce W. Menning. The State Military Publishing House of the USSR People's Defense Commissariat: Moscow, 1937.

Galula, David. *Counterinsurgency Warfare: Theory and Practice*. St. Petersburg: Hailer Publishing, 2005.

Gordon, Michael R., and General Bernard E. Trainor. *The Generals' War : The Inside Story of the Conflict in the Gulf*. Boston: Back Bay Books, 1995.

Gray, Colin S. *War, Peace and International Relations: An Introduction to Strategic History*. New York: Routledge, 2008.

Gregg, Heather S., Hy S. Rothstein, and John Arquilla, eds. *The Three Circles of War: Understanding the Dynamics of Conflict in Iraq*. Washington, D.C.: Potomac Books Inc., 2010.

Kelly, Justin and Mike Brennan. *Alien: How Operational Art Devoured Strategy*. Strategic Studies Institute Monographs. Carlisle Barracks, PA: U.S. Army War College, 2009.

Kilcullen, David. *The Accidental Guerrilla: Fighting Small Wars in the Midst of a Big One*. Oxford: Oxford University Press, USA, 2009.

Kilcullen, David. "Counter-insurgency Redux." *Survival* 48, no. 4 (Winter 2006-2007): 111-130.

Kirkpatrick, Charles E..*An Unknown Future and a Doubtful Present: Writing the Victory Plan of 1941*.Washington: Center of Military History, 1992.

Kuehl, Dale. "Inside the Surge: 1-5 Cavalry in Ameriyah." *Small Wars Journal* (14 March 2011): http://smallwarsjournal.com (accessed March 21, 2011).

Krause, Michael D. and R. Cody Phillips. *Historical Perspectives of the Operational Art*. Washington, D.C.: United States Army Center for Military History, 2007.

Linn, Brian McAllister. *The Echo of Battle: The Army's Way of War*. Cambridge, MA: Harvard University Press, 2007.

Murray, Williamson A. "The Industrialization of War 1815-71." In *The Cambridge Illustrated History of Warfare*, by Geoffrey Parker. Cambridge: Cambridge University Press, 2008.

Mockaitis, Thomas R. *Iraq and the Challenge of Counterinsurgency.* Westport: Praeger, 2008.

Napoleoni, Loretta. *Insurgent Iraq: Al-Zarqawi and the New Generation.* New York: Seven Stories Press, 2005.

Naveh, Shimon, Jim Schneider and Timothy Challans. *The Structure of Operational Revolution: A Prolegomena.* Leavenworth: Booz Allen Hamilton Inc., 2009

Naveh, Shimon. *In Pursuit of Military Excellence: The Evolution of Operational Theory.* London: Frank Cass, 1997.

Newell, Clayton R. and Michael D. Krause. *On Operational Art.* Washington, D.C.: Antulio J. Echevarria II. *Clausewitz & Contemporary War.* New York: Oxford University Press, 2007.

Parsa, Misagh. States, *Ideologies, & Social Revolutions.* Cambridge, UK: Cambridge University Press, 2000.

Phillips, Cody. *Historical Perspectives of the Operational Art.* Washington, D.C.: United States Army Center for Military History, 2007.

Ricks, Thomas E. *The Gamble: General David Petraeus and the American Military Adventure in Iraq, 2006-2008.* 1St Edition ed. New York: Penguin Press HC, 2009.

Robinson, Linda. *Tell Me How This Ends: General David Petraeus and the Search for a Way Out of Iraq.* New York: PublicAffairs, 2008.

Schneider, James R. *Theoretical Paper No. Three. The Theory of Operational Art.* Fort Leavenworth: United States Army Command and General Staff College, 1 March 1988

Schneider, James R. *Theoretical Paper No. Four. Vulcan's Anvil: The American Civil War and the Foundation of Operational Art.* Fort Leavenworth: United States Army Command and General Staff College, 10 May 2004

Simpson, Brooks D. *Ulysses S. Grant: Triumph Over Adversity, 1822-1865.* Boston: Houghton Mifflin Harcourt, 2000.

Smith, Rupert. *The Utility of Force: The Art of War in the Modern World.* New York: Vintage, 2008

Swain, Richard M. *"Lucky War" Third Army in Desert Storm.* Fort Leavenworth, KS: U.S. Army Command and General Staff College Press, 1994

Swain, Richard M. "Filling the Void: The Operational Art and the U.S. Army." In *Operational Art: Developments in the Theory of War*, edited by B.J.C. McKercher and Michael Hennessy. Westport, CT: Praeger, 1996.

Van Creveld, Martin. *Command in War.* Cambridge: Harvard University Press, 1985.

Wass de Czege, Huba. "Thinking and Acting Like an Explorer: Operational Art Is Not a Level of War." *Small Wars Journal* (14 March 2011): http://smallwarsjournal.com (accessed March 21, 2011).

JP 5-0: Joint Operations Planning. U.S. Department of Defense Joint Publication (JP). Washington, DC: U.S. Department of Defense, 2006.

JP 3-0: Joint Operations. U.S. Department of Defense Joint Publication (JP). Washington, DC: U.S. Department of Defense, 2008.

FM 3-0: Operations. U.S. Dept. of the Army Field Manual (FM). Washington, DC: U.S. Department of the Army, 2008.

FM 3-24: Counterinsurgency. U.S. Dept. of the Army Field Manual (FM). Washington, DC: U.S. Department of the Army, 2006.

FM 5-0: Army Planning and Orders Production. U.S. Dept. of the Army Field Manual (FM). Washington, DC: U.S. Department of the Army, 2010.

FM 100-5 (OBSOLETE): *Operations.* U.S. Dept. of the Army Field Manual (FM). Washington, DC: U.S. Department of the Army, 1986.

FM 100-5 (OBSOLETE): *Operations.* U.S. Dept. of the Army Field Manual (FM). Washington, DC: U.S. Department of the Army, 1982.